The Next Hundred Lears

Limericks After Lear

Book Two

John Arthur Nichol
Illustrations by Rory Walker

Text Copyright © John Arthur Nichol 2020

Illustrations Copyright © Rory Walker 2020

All Rights Reserved

Edward Lear's verses are in the public domain.

ISBN
978-0-6489059-4-3 (paperback)
978-0-6489059-3-6 (EPUB)

 A catalogue record for this work is available from the National Library of Australia

Cover Illustration Copyright © Rory Walker 2020

For Dave, Jeff and Pete. Always.

Contents

The Limericks *15*
A Person of Bantry *16*
A Man at a Junction *18*
A Person of Minety *19*
A Man of Thermopylae *20*
A Person of Deal *21*
A Man of the Humber *22*
A Man In a Barge *23*
A Man of Dunrose *24*
A Man of Toulouse *25*
A Person of Bree *26*
A Person of Bromley *28*
A Person of Shields *29*
A Man of Dunluce *30*
A Man of Deeside *31*

A Person in Black *32*

A Man of the Dargle *33*

A Person of Pinner *34*

A Person of China *35*

A Man in a Marsh *36*

A Person of Brill *37*

A Person of Wick *38*

A Man At a Station *39*

A Man of Three Bridges *40*

A Man of Hong Kong *42*

A Person in Green *43*

A Person of Fife *44*

A Man Who Screamed Out *45*

A Lady in White *46*

A Person of Slough *47*

A Person of Down *48*

A Person in Red *49*

A Person of Hove *50*

A Person in Pink *51*

A Lady of France *53*

A Person of Putney *54*

A Person of Loo *55*

A Person of Woking *56*

A Person of Dean *57*

A Lady in Blue *59*

A Man in a Garden *60*

A Person of Pisa *61*

A Person of Florence *62*

A Person of Sheen *63*

A Person of Ware *64*

A Person of Janina *65*

A Man of Cashmere *67*

A Person of Cassel *68*

A Person of Pett *69*

A Man of Spithead *70*

A Man on the Border *71*

A Man of Dumbree *72*

A Person of Filey *73*

A Man Whose Remorse *74*

A Man of Ibreem *75*

A Person of Wilts *76*

A Person of Grange *77*

A Person of Newry *78*

A Man of Dumblane *79*

A Man of Port Grigor *80*

A Man of El Hums *81*

A Man of West Dumpet *83*

A Person of Sark *84*

A Man Whose Despair *85*

A Person of Barnes *86*

A Person of Nice *87*

A Lady of Greenwich *88*

A Person of Cannes *89*

A Person of Ickley *90*

A Person of Hyde *91*

A Person in Grey *92*

A Man of Ancona *93*

A Person of Sestri *95*

A Person of Blythe *96*

A Person of Ayr *97*

A Person of Rimini *98*

A Lady, Whose Nose *99*

A Person of Eling *100*

A Man of Thames Ditton *101*

A Person of Bray *102*

A Person Whose History *103*

A Person of Bow *104*

A Person of Rye *105*

A Person of Crowle *106*

A Lady of Winchelsea *107*

A Man In a Tree *108*

A Lady of Corsica *110*

A Lady of Firle *111*

A Person of Stroud *112*

A Man of Boulak *113*

A Person of Skye *114*

A Man of Blackheath *115*

A Man, Who When Little *116*

A Person of Dundalk *117*

A Person of Shoreham *118*

A Person of Bar *119*

A Person of Kew *120*

A Person of Jodd *121*

A Person of Bude *122*

A Person of Brigg *123*

A Man of Messina *124*
The Fifth Line *126*
Sascha Martin's Rocket-Ship *128*
Thank You *131*

Illustrations

There was a Young Lady of Bantry 17

There was a Young Lady of Bree 27

A Painterly Man of Three Bridges 41

There was a Young Lady in Pink 52

A Man in the Forest of Dean 58

There was a Young Lady, Janina 66

In the Fictional Place of El Hums 82

There was a Small Dog in Ancona 94

There was an Old Man in a Tree 109

Police Came and Got the Hyaena 125

Foreword

In 1872 Edward Lear published a new book - *More Nonsense Pictures, Rhymes, Botany, etc.*. It included *One Hundred Nonsense Pictures And Rhymes* - a hundred new limericks closely modelled on the verses that had done so well for Lear in *A Book of Nonsense*.

These new limericks represent the third wave of Lear's venture in the form.

The first was in 1846, when he published *A Book of Nonsense*.

The second was in 1863, when *A Book of Nonsense, to Which is Added More Nonsense*, became a bestseller, launching the limerick on a journey that would continue through the turn of two centuries.

Lear's third wave was barely a ripple.

Coming nine years after his great success, the verses in *One Hundred Nonsense Pictures and Rhymes* caused no excitement. If they were read at all, they were quickly forgotten, along with Lear's formula that discarded the most powerful element in a limerick's line-up: the fifth line.

The limerick itself had moved on, with a strict set of rules defining a form that, paradoxically, could take on any thought a human being might entertain.

In *The Fifth Line*, I created 112 new limericks from the bones of *A Book of Nonsense*. I called it *The Fifth Line* because that was the part of the limerick - the heart of the limerick - that Lear had cast out, and that I wanted to restore.

In this second volume, *The Next Hundred Lears*, I've revived all of Lear's 1872 originals and paired them with my own new verses. At times I draw clearly on the source; at others, I barely reference it. I'm fond of some, and less fond of others. Limericks are always a work in progress.

But they're also an entertainment, and I hope that, in *The Next Hundred Lears*, you'll find a genuine smile or two :)

John Arthur Nichol, Sydney, 2020

The Limericks

Verse One, every page after here,
Is a '72 Edward Lear,
And the Second Verse then
Is by me, John A N,
In the twenty-first twentieth year.

A Person of Bantry

There was a Young Person of Bantry,
Who frequently slept in the pantry;
When disturbed by the mice, she appeased
them with rice,
That judicious Young Person of Bantry.

Edward Lear

There was a Young Person of Bantry,
Who frequently slept in the pantry,
After throwing a tanter
At all of the banter
And singing that came from the chantry.

There was a Young Lady of Bantry

A Man at a Junction

There was an Old Man at a Junction,
Whose feelings were wrung with compunction
When they said, "The Train's gone!" he
exclaimed, "How forlorn!"
But remained on the rails of the Junction.

Edward Lear

A Fellow, applying an unction,
Found something amiss in its function:
When attacking a blemish
It rendered him Flemish
And sent him to Ghent, in conjunction.

A Person of Minety

There was an Old Person of Minety,
Who purchased five hundred and ninety
Large apples and pears, which he threw
unawares
At the heads of the people of Minety.

Edward Lear

There was an Old Saxon in Myntey
Whose helmet was battered and dinty;
So he put one on lay-by,
The total to pay by
July, seven hundred and twinty.

A Man of Thermopylae

There was an Old Man of Thermopylae,
Who never did anything properly;
But they said, "If you choose to boil eggs in
your shoes,
You shall never remain in Thermopylae."

Edward Lear

There was an Old Man of Thermopylae
Who was rich from a cooking monopoly,
Using footwear as cookware
That hung on a hook where
He'd finally done something properly.

A Person of Deal

There was an Old Person of Deal,
Who in walking used only his heel;
When they said, "Tell us why?" he made no reply,
That mysterious Old Person of Deal.

Edward Lear

There was an Old Person of Deal,
Who didn't believe he was real;
And the world, as a vision,
He viewed with derision,
But that in itself was surreal.

A Man of the Humber

There was an Old Man on the Humber,
Who dined on a cake of Burnt Umber;
When he said, "It's enough!" they only said,
"Stuff!
You amazing Old Man on the Humber!"

Edward Lear

A Man had a house on the Humber,
In its shape a misshapen cucumber;
And they christened it "Winnie"
Because (what a ninny!)
He'd painted his dwelling in umber.

A Man In a Barge

There was an Old Man in a Barge,
Whose nose was exceedingly large;
But in fishing by night, it supported a light,
Which helped that Old Man in a barge.

Edward Lear

There was an Old Man on a Charge:
"Sir, this fart you released on a barge,
Wasn't meant, you deny it,
To foster a riot?"
"Milord, it was more an homage."

A Man of Dunrose

There was an Old Man of Dunrose;
A parrot seized hold of his nose.
When he grew melancholy, they said, "His
name's Polly,"
Which soothed that Old Man of Dunrose.

Edward Lear

There was an Old Man of Dunrose
Who couldn't get windows to close;
His defences were thin
When the outside came in,
And a parrot took hold of his nose.

A Man of Toulouse

There was an Old Man of Toulouse
Who purchased a new pair of shoes;
When they asked, "Are they pleasant?" he
said, "Not at present!"
That turbid Old Man of Toulouse.

Edward Lear

There was an Old Man of Toulouse
Who gathered a gaggle of flus,
And an interesting virus
That came from Epirus
With hundreds of happy reviews.

A Person of Bree

There was an Old Person of Bree,
Who frequented the depths of the sea;
She nurs'd the small fishes, and washed all the dishes,
And swam back again into Bree.

Edward Lear

There was a Young Lady of Bree
Whose sleep was disturbed by a pea;
It was under her bed,
And it suddenly said
That it fancied a muffin and tea.

There was a Young Lady of Bree

A Person of Bromley

There was an Old Person of Bromley,
Whose ways were not cheerful or comely;
He sate in the dust, eating spiders and crust,
That unpleasing Old Person of Bromley.

Edward Lear

There was a Young Lady of Bromley
Rolling eyes and enduring a hom'ly
From her dad, in full flight
On the perils of night,
And she wished it were just an anom'ly.

A Person of Shields

There was an Old Person of Shields,
Who frequented the vallies and fields;
All the mice and the cats, and the snakes and the rats,
Followed after that person of Shields.

Edward Lear

"I'm the Beast, and the Beast never yields!"
Said the Beast to a man in the fields;
But the Beast had to go
Without landing a blow,
For his foe was a Person of Shields.

A Man of Dunluce

There was an Old Man of Dunluce,
Who went out to sea on a goose:
When he'd gone out a mile, he observ'd with a smile,
"It is time to return to Dunluce."

Edward Lear

There was an Old Man of Dunluce,
Who shouldn't have ever got loose;
But he summoned his minions
From other dominions,
And made his escape on a goose.

A Man of Deeside

*There was an Old Man of Deeside
Whose hat was exceedingly wide,
But he said, "Do not fail, if it happen to hail,
To come under my hat at Deeside!"*

Edward Lear

*A Fellow who lived by the Dee
Heard that life was all right by the sea;
So when told of the seaside,
The Fellow from Deeside,
Set off to the seaside to see.*

A Person in Black

There was an Old Person in black,
A Grasshopper jumped on his back;
When it chirped in his ear, he was smitten with fear,
That helpless Old Person in black.

Edward Lear

There was a Young Lady in Black ...
A grasshopper jumped on her snack
As the girl, unaware,
Bit the succulent fare,
With a crunch and a squish and a crack.

A Man of the Dargle

There was an Old Man of the Dargle
Who purchased six barrels of Gargle;
For he said, "I'll sit still, and will roll them down hill,
For the fish in the depths of the Dargle."

Edward Lear

There was an Old Man of the Dargle
Who wanted his parrot to gargle;
So he held it upright
With its beak open tight,
And of course it was just a debagle.

A Person of Pinner

There was an Old Person of Pinner,
As thin as a lath, if not thinner;
They dressed him in white, and roll'd him up tight,
That elastic Old Person of Pinner.

Edward Lear

There was a Young Person of Pinner,
Who in spite of her charming deminour,
Had a focus infernal
Upon the internal,
And wouldn't come down for her dinner.

A Person of China

There was an Old Person of China,
Whose daughters were Jiska and Dinah,
Amelia and Fluffy, Olivia and Chuffy,
And all of them settled in China.

Edward Lear

A somnolent person of China
Lay trapped in an awkward recliner;
He was folded up inter
The storage for Winter,
And stayed till the weather was finer.

A Man in a Marsh

There was an Old Man in a Marsh,
Whose manners were futile and harsh;
He sate on a log, and sang songs to a frog,
That instructive Old Man in a Marsh.

Edward Lear

A frog sat opposed, in a marsh,
To a toad, whose expression was harsh,
While the man who'd arranged them
Artistically changed them,
And captured the scene in gouache.

A Person of Brill

There was an Old Person of Brill,
Who purchased a shirt with a frill;
But they said, "Don't you wish, you mayn't
look like a fish,
You obsequious Old Person of Brill?"

Edward Lear

There was an Old Person of Brill,
Who sat most alarmingly still;
When they said, "Are you dead?"
He just nodded his head,
And the wailing began with a will.

A Person of Wick

*There was an Old Person of Wick,
Who said, "Tick-a-Tick, Tick-a-Tick;
Chickabee, Chickabaw." And he said nothing
more,
That laconic Old Person of Wick.*

Edward Lear

*There was a Young Lady of Wick,
Who woke every day with a hic;
But a lick up of tea
Fixed the hic up and she
Was about on all fours in a tick.*

A Man At a Station

There was an Old Man at a Station,
Who made a promiscuous oration;
But they said, "Take some snuff!—You have talk'd quite enough,
You afflicting Old Man at a Station!"

Edward Lear

An orator down at the Station,
Would always expand on inflation,
And the ruinous helium-
Filled epithelium
Found in the heads of the nation.

A Man of Three Bridges

There was an Old Man of Three Bridges,
Whose mind was distracted by midges,
He sate on a wheel, eating underdone veal,
Which relieved that Old Man of Three Bridges.

Edward Lear

A painterly man of Three Bridges
Did a blistering vista of squidges;
And he couldn't but smirk
At demand for the work,
Cause he'd only been squishing the midges.

A Painterly Man of Three Bridges

A Man of Hong Kong

There was an Old Man of Hong Kong,
Who never did anything wrong;
He lay on his back, with his head in a sack,
That innocuous Old Man of Hong Kong.

Edward Lear

There was an Old Man in Hong Kong
With a sense that he didn't belong;
For it filled him with fear
Having anyone near,
And he always went out in a throng.

A Person in Green

There was a Young Person in Green,
Who seldom was fit to be seen;
She wore a long shawl, over bonnet and all,
Which enveloped that person in green.

Edward Lear

There was a Young Girl Who, in Green,
Would be muddled and fuddled and mean;
But she'd flow, when in yellow,
From angry to mellow,
And sample the bits in between.

A Person of Fife

There was an Old Person of Fife,
Who was greatly disgusted with life;
They sang him a ballad, and fed him on salad,
Which cured that Old Person of Fife.

Edward Lear

There was a Young Fellow of Fife,
Where hatred of music was rife;
So he went to Glamorgan
To play on an organ
And barely escaped with his life.

A Man Who Screamed Out

There was an Old Man who screamed out
Whenever they knocked him about:
So they took off his boots, and fed him with fruits,
And continued to knock him about.

Edward Lear

There was a Young Lady who dreamed
That she looked in the mirror and screamed;
In the light of the dawn
She was haggard and worn,
And she looked in the mirror and screamed.

A Lady in White

There was a Young Lady in White,
Who looked out at the depths of the night;
But the birds of the air, filled her heart with despair,
And oppressed that Young Lady in white.

Edward Lear

There was a Young Lady in White,
Who looked out at the depths of the night;
Then, dressing in black
As she slipped out the back,
She gave Chinky the Pixie a fright.

A Person of Slough

There was an Old Person of Slough,
Who danced at the end of a bough;
But they said, "If you sneeze, you might
damage the trees,
You imprudent Old Person of Slough."

Edward Lear

There was an Old Person of Slough,
Who climbed to the end of a bough;
It was scary, by gad,
But he knew that he had
To go out there and rescue his cow.

A Person of Down

There was an Old Person of Down,
Whose face was adorned with a frown;
When he opened the door, for one minute or more,
He alarmed all the people of Down.

Edward Lear

There was an Old Person of Down,
Who was seventh in line to the Crown;
But he went for a wee
When the toilet was free ...
Now he's seventy ninth, with a frown.

A Person in Red

There was a Young Person in red,
Who carefully covered her head,
With a bonnet of leather, and three lines of feather,
Besides some long ribands of red.

   Edward Lear

The Number Three Lady in Red
Had an elegant thought in her head,
That by dressing in Blue
She could be Number Two,
Or the Number One Purple instead.

A Person of Hove

There was an Old Person of Hove,
Who frequented the depths of a grove;
Where he studied his books, with the wrens and
the rooks,
That tranquil Old Person of Hove.

Edward Lear

There was a Young Lady of Hove,
Who swam in a pretty blue cove,
With a porpoise, a turtle,
A friend (who was Myrtle),
And mantas in yellow and mauve.

A Person in Pink

There was a Young Person in Pink,
Who called out for something to drink;
But they said, "O my daughter, there's nothing but water!"
Which vexed that Young Person in pink.

Edward Lear

There was a Young Lady in Pink,
Who rode on a galloping skink;
It was green and they clashed,
And her outfit was trashed,
But she'd do it again in a wink.

There was a Young Lady in Pink

A Lady of France

There was an Old Lady of France,
Who taught little ducklings to dance;
When she said, "Tick-a-tack!" they only said,
"Quack!"
Which grieved that Old Lady of France.

Edward Lear

There was an Old Person of France
Who had such a way with the plants;
They'd be ever so still
As he'd water and till,
And you'd swear they were all in a trance.

A Person of Putney

*There was an Old Person of Putney,
Whose food was roast spiders and chutney,
Which he took with his tea, within sight of the sea,
That romantic Old Person of Putney.*

Edward Lear

*There was an Old Person of Putney
Who had to hold fire on his glutt'ny
When they gave him a bustard
With dollops of mustard,
Instead of a chicken and chutney.*

A Person of Loo

There was an Old Person of Loo,
Who said, "What on earth shall I do?"
When they said, "Go away!" she continued to stay,
That vexatious Old Person of Loo.

Edward Lear

There was an Old Person of Loo,
Letting animals out of the zoo;
And the pigeons he stirred
To rebel, with a word,
So they took the Town Hall in a coo.

A Person of Woking

There was an Old Person of Woking,
Whose mind was perverse and provoking;
He sate on a rail, with his head in a pail,
That illusive Old Person of Woking.

Edward Lear

There was a Young Person of Woking,
Who spent a whole morning provoking;
When he did get a bite
It just gave him a fright,
And his trousers a bit of a soaking.

A Person of Dean

*There was an Old Person of Dean
Who dined on one pea, and one bean;
For he said, "More than that, would make me too fat,"
That cautious Old Person of Dean.*

Edward Lear

*A man in the Forest of Dean
Was waylaid by a pea and a bean;
They said, "Stand and deliver!"
And rattled a quiver
Of arrows, and both were in green.*

A Man in the Forest of Dean

A Lady in Blue

There was a Young Lady in Blue,
Who said, "Is it you? Is it you?"
When they said, "Yes, it is," she replied only,
"Whizz!"
That ungracious Young Lady in blue.

Edward Lear

There was a Young Lady in Blue,
Who said, "Is it you? Is it you?"
"No it's not, it is I,"
Came the earnest reply,
And she couldn't decide what to do.

A Man in a Garden

*There was an old Man in a Garden,
Who always begged every one's pardon;
When they asked him, "What for?" he replied,
"You're a bore!
And I trust you'll go out of my garden."*

Edward Lear

*There was an old Man in a Garden
Who belched, then requested the pardon
Of a butterfly there
As it faced him, to stare,
Its expression beginning to harden.*

A Person of Pisa

There was an Old Person of Pisa,
Whose daughters did nothing to please her;
She dressed them in grey, and banged them all day,
Round the walls of the city of Pisa.

Edward Lear

There was a Young Person of Pisa
Who'd sneeze when the fancy would seize her
To indulge in a bite
Of forbidden delight,
Cause she hid all the treats in the freezer.

A Person of Florence

There was an Old Person of Florence,
Who held mutton chops in abhorrence;
He purchased a Bustard, and fried him in
Mustard,
Which choked that Old Person of Florence.

Edward Lear

There was a Young Person of Florence,
Whose elders he viewed with abhorrence;
They were boring and grave
And knew nothing, but gave
Him advice in unstoppable torrents.

A Person of Sheen

There was an Old Person of Sheen,
Whose expression was calm and serene;
He sate in the water, and drank bottled porter,
That placid Old Person of Sheen.

Edward Lear

There was an Old Person of Sheen
Who'd bounce on a big trampoline
After dinner each night;
It was not for delight
But to settle his English cuisine.

A Person of Ware

There was an Old Person of Ware,
Who rode on the back of a bear;
When they ask'd, "Does it trot?" he said,
"Certainly not!
He's a Moppsikon Floppsikon bear!"

  Edward Lear

There was an Old Person of Ware
Who initially sat on a bear,
But recalling, in Riga,
The girl and the tiger,
Dismounted and boarded a hare.

A Person of Janina

There was a Young Person of Janina,
Whose uncle was always a fanning her;
When he fanned off her head, she smiled
sweetly, and said,
"You propitious Old Person of Janina!"

Edward Lear

There was a Young Lady, Janina,
Who was sent to the Roman arena;
She escaped, it is said,
With the Emperor's head,
And his absolute favourite hyaena.

There was a Young Lady, Janina

A Man of Cashmere

There was an Old Man of Cashmere,
Whose movements were scroobious and queer;
Being slender and tall, he looked over a wall,
And perceived two fat ducks of Cashmere.

Edward Lear

There was an Old Man of Cashmere,
Whose manner was cold and austere;
But he'd fall in a heap
And would giggle and squeak
If you happened to blow in his ear.

A Person of Cassel

There was an Old Person of Cassel,
Whose nose finished off in a tassel;
But they call'd out, "Oh well! don't it look like
a bell!"
Which perplexed that Old Person of Cassel.

Edward Lear

There was an Old Person of Cassel
Whose daring new use of a tassel
As a luridly odd piece
Attached to his cod-piece
Had made him the talk of the castle.

A Person of Pett

There was an Old Person of Pett,
Who was partly consumed by regret;
He sate in a cart, and ate cold apple tart,
Which relieved that Old Person of Pett.

Edward Lear

There was an Old Woman of Pett
Whose lingering note of regret
As she sat on a tart
In a runaway cart
Was a sound they would never forget.

A Man of Spithead

There was an Old Man of Spithead,
Who opened the window, and said,—
"Fil-jomble, fil-jumble, fil-rumble-come-
tumble!"
That doubtful Old Man of Spithead.

Edward Lear

There was an Old Man of Spithead
Who lay on the floor as if dead,
Then, in idle depravity,
Switching the gravity,
Lay on the ceiling instead.

A Man on the Border

There was an Old Man on the Border,
Who lived in the utmost disorder;
He danced with the cat, and made tea in his hat,
Which vexed all the folks on the Border.

Edward Lear

There was an Old Man on the Border
Who wasn't an order applauder,
So he moved to a state
With a lot on its plate
And a border in broader disorder.

A Man of Dumbree

*There was an Old Man of Dumbree,
Who taught little owls to drink tea;
For he said, "To eat mice is not proper or nice,"
That amiable man of Dumbree.*

Edward Lear

*There was an Old Man of Dumbree,
Who couldn't say no to High Tea,
And would stay at the teahouse
Up there in the treehouse
Till nearly a quarter to three.*

A Person of Filey

There was an Old Person of Filey,
Of whom his acquaintance spoke highly;
He danced perfectly well, to the sound of a bell,
And delighted the people of Filey.

Edward Lear

There was an Old Dentist of Filey
Who greeted his patients all smiley,
Because making a killing
Was truly fulfilling,
He found, and he valued it highly.

A Man Whose Remorse

*There was an Old Man whose remorse
Induced him to drink Caper Sauce;
For they said, "If mixed up with some cold claret-cup,
It will certainly soothe your remorse!"*

Edward Lear

*A Bloodthirsty Man of the Norse
Felt a deep and unwonted remorse
For the raid in review,
Cause he'd ruined his do
By ensnaring his hair in the gorse.*

A Man of Ibreem

There was an Old Man of Ibreem,
Who suddenly threaten'd to scream;
But they said, "If you do, we will thump you
quite blue,
You disgusting Old Man of Ibreem!"

Edward Lear

There was an Old Man of Ibreem
Who lived in a fissure of steam;
As extremophiles go
This is nothing, although
It was tough on his peaches and cream.

A Person of Wilts

There was an Old Person of Wilts,
Who constantly walked upon stilts;
He wreathed them with lilies and daffy-down-
dillies,
That elegant person of Wilts.

Edward Lear

There was a Young Person of Wilts,
Who had an attack of the guilts,
After sacking the wardrobe
Of Grandmother Ord' Robe
And shortening all of her stilts.

A Person of Grange

There was an Old Person of Grange,
Whose manners were scroobious and strange;
He sailed to St. Blubb in a waterproof tub,
That aquatic Old Person of Grange.

Edward Lear

There was an Old Person of Grange,
Whose mood was increasingly strange:
He'd been feeling depressed
Since he'd moved to the West,
And he wasn't at home on the range.

A Person of Newry

There was an Old Person of Newry,
Whose manners were tinctured with fury;
He tore all the rugs, and broke all the jugs,
Within twenty miles' distance of Newry.

Edward Lear

There was an Old Person of Newry,
Who purchased a Plymouth in Bury,
It was zippy and snappy
And oh, he was happy
To drive around town in a Fury.

A Man of Dumblane

There was an Old Man of Dumblane,
Who greatly resembled a crane;
But they said, "Is it wrong, since your legs are so long,
To request you won't stay in Dumblane?"

  Edward Lear

There was an Old Man of Dumblane
Who was always so pallid and vain;
When they said he was flushed,
He could well have been crushed,
But he thought they were pulling his chain.

A Man of Port Grigor

There was an Old Man of Port Grigor,
Whose actions were noted for vigour;
He stood on his head till his waistcoat turned red,
That eclectic Old Man of Port Grigor.

Edward Lear

There was an Old Man of Port Grigor,
Whose finger was poised on the trigger
Of competitive eating,
And victories fleeting
That threatened to ruin his figure.

A Man of El Hums

There was an Old Man of El Hums,
Who lived upon nothing but crumbs,
Which he picked off the ground, with the other birds round,
In the roads and the lanes of El Hums.

Edward Lear

In the Fictional Place of El Hums
Lived a man who existed on crumbs;
But on Sunday he'd sup
(Since we're making it up)
On a Pterosaur garnished with plums.

In the Fictional Place of El Hums

A Man of West Dumpet

There was an Old Man of West Dumpet,
Who possessed a large nose like a trumpet;
When he blew it aloud, it astonished the crowd,
And was heard through the whole of West
Dumpet.

Edward Lear

There was an Old Man of West Dumpet,
Who'd set up a hurdle and jump it,
Then saunter inside
With a feeling of pride,
Cause he knew he'd made room for a crumpet.

A Person of Sark

There was an Old Person of Sark,
Who made an unpleasant remark;
But they said, "Don't you see what a brute you must be,
You obnoxious Old Person of Sark!"

Edward Lear

There was an Old Person of Sark,
Who made an unpleasant remark;
But his friend, Miss Perfectron,
Who'd shed an electron,
Said, "Try to be positive, Mark."

A Man Whose Despair

There was an Old Man whose despair
Induced him to purchase a hare:
Whereon one fine day he rode wholly away,
Which partly assuaged his despair.

Edward Lear

There was an Old Man whose despair
Caused his body to rise in the air,
And it banished the gloom,
So he fell to his doom,
Because life can be pretty unfair.

A Person of Barnes

*There was an Old Person of Barnes,
Whose garments were covered with darns;
But they said, "Without doubt, you will soon wear them out,
You luminous person of Barnes!"*

Edward Lear

*There was an Old Person of Barnes,
A show-off, returning from Cannes,
Whose repeated "Mais oui?"
Was confusing, and he
Wouldn't stop saying "quarante" and "quinze."*

A Person of Nice

There was an Old Person of Nice,
Whose associates were usually Geese.
They walked out together in all sorts of
weather,
That affable person of Nice!

Edward Lear

There was an Old Person of Nice,
Whose friends were a gaggle of geese;
They were pleasantly honky
But morally shonky,
And given to acts of caprice.

A Lady of Greenwich

There was a Young Lady of Greenwich,
Whose garments were border'd with Spinach;
But a large spotty Calf bit her shawl quite in half,
Which alarmed that Young Lady of Greenwich.

Edward Lear

There was a Young Lady of Greenwich,
Who managed a seven to ten itch;
But she wanted eleven
And that would be heaven
Cause then she ascended to Zen Itch.

A Person of Cannes

There was an Old Person of Cannes,
Who purchased three fowls and a fan;
Those she placed on a stool, and to make them feel cool
She constantly fanned them at Cannes.

Edward Lear

There was a Young Person of Cannes,
Who lived on a boat with his gran;
He could do his own thing
Cause he had his own wing -
That's a thing, on a catamaran.

A Person of Ickley

There was an Old Person of Ickley,
Who could not abide to ride quickly;
He rode to Karnak on a tortoise's back,
That moony Old Person of Ickley.

Edward Lear

There was a Big Tortoise of Ickley
Whose shell was appallingly prickly,
So the man who would ride it,
Instead, walked beside it,
And never got anywhere quickly.

A Person of Hyde

There was an Old Person of Hyde,
Who walked by the shore with his bride,
Till a Crab who came near fill'd their bosoms with fear,
And they said, "Would we'd never left Hyde!"

Edward Lear

There was a Young Lady of Hyde
Who was always washed out on the tide;
Though she'd studied the lore
Of the treacherous shore,
It was knowledge she'd never applied.

A Person in Grey

There was an Old Person in Grey,
Whose feelings were tinged with dismay;
She purchased two parrots, and fed them with carrots,
Which pleased that Old Person in grey.

Edward Lear

There was a Young Lady in Grey
Who'd frolic and gambol and play;
She was happy and bright
At the height of the night,
But resented the start of the day.

A Man of Ancona

There was an Old Man of Ancona,
Who found a small dog with no owner,
Which he took up and down all the streets of
the town,
That anxious Old Man of Ancona.

Edward Lear

There was a Small Dog in Ancona
Who found an Old Man with no owner;
So he rounded him up
And was asked by a pup,
"Is he yours?" "No, he's only a loaner."

There was a Small Dog in Ancona

A Person of Sestri

There was an Old Person of Sestri,
Who sate himself down in the vestry;
When they said, "You are wrong!" he merely
said "Bong!"
That repulsive Old Person of Sestri.

Edward Lear

There was an Old Person of Sestri,
Whose seizures (Italian: sequestri)
Turned him into a fly,
And he couldn't say why,
But he tended to change in the vestry.

A Person of Blythe

There was an Old Person of Blythe,
Who cut up his meat with a scythe;
When they said, "Well! I never!" he cried,
"Scythes for ever!"
That lively Old Person of Blythe.

Edward Lear

There was a Young Lady of Blythe
Who kept a retractable scythe
In the depths of a pocket,
But couldn't quite lock it,
And tended to wriggle and writhe.

A Person of Ayr

There was a Young Person of Ayr,
Whose head was remarkably square:
On the top, in fine weather, she wore a gold
feather;
Which dazzled the people of Ayr.

Edward Lear

There was a Young Lady of Ayr,
Whose rapid ascent was unfair,
Being down to genetics;
It wasn't aesthetics,
But rather, her flyaway hair.

A Person of Rimini

*There was an Old Person of Rimini,
Who said, "Gracious! Goodness! O Gimini!"
When they said, "Please be still!" she ran down a hill,
And was never more heard of at Rimini.*

Edward Lear

*It's disarmingly calming in Rimini,
But it hosts an alarming acrimony,
For the homes of a few
Are of silver, right through,
But the others are made of antimony.*

A Lady, Whose Nose

There is a Young Lady, Whose Nose,
Continually prospers and grows;
When it grew out of sight, she exclaimed in a
fright,
"Oh! Farewell to the end of my nose!"

Edward Lear

There was a Young Lady Whose Nose
Really suited her face where it rose;
It was quite the delight
As a stationary sight,
But when running was not, I suppose.

A Person of Eling

There was an Old Person of Ealing,
Who was wholly devoid of good feeling;
He drove a small gig, with three Owls and a
Pig,
Which distressed all the people of Ealing.

Edward Lear

A Pondering Person of Eling,
Hung deeply in thought from the ceiling;
But a brilliant idea
Put him flat on his ear,
So he would have been better off kneeling.

A Man of Thames Ditton

There was an Old Man of Thames Ditton,
Who called out for something to sit on;
But they brought him a hat, and said, "Sit upon that,
You abruptious Old Man of Thames Ditton!"

Edward Lear

There was an Old Man of Thames Ditton
Whose two middle fingers were bitten,
Cause he'd left them extended
And gravely offended
A visiting Primate of Britain.

A Person of Bray

There was an Old Person of Bray,
Who sang through the whole of the day
To his ducks and his pigs, whom he fed upon figs,
That valuable person of Bray.

Edward Lear

There was an Old Person of Bray,
Whose cat wouldn't talk for a day;
Although breakfast was served
With the grace it deserved,
It was not on its favourite tray.

A Person Whose History

There was a Young Person Whose History
Was always considered a mystery;
She sate in a ditch, although no one knew which,
And composed a small treatise on history.

Edward Lear

There was a Young Lady Whose History
Offered up a remarkable mystery:
Why on earth would she choose
Such unsuitable shoes
That her feet were all twisted and blistery?

A Person of Bow

There was an Old Person of Bow,
Whom nobody happened to know;
So they gave him some soap, and said coldly,
"We hope
You will go back directly to Bow!"

   Edward Lear

A Fanatical Vegan from Bow
And an Omnivore (wouldn't you know?)
Walked into a bar,
And the tender said, "Ah,
You'll have come for the smorgasbord, no?"

A Person of Rye

There was an Old Person of Rye,
Who went up to town on a fly;
But they said, "If you cough, you are safe to
fall off!
You abstemious Old Person of Rye!"

Edward Lear

There was an Old Writer of Rye
Who wrote all his books on the fly;
But a baking aroma
Put fly in a coma,
And all of his proof in the pie.

A Person of Crowle

There was an Old Person of Crowle,
Who lived in the nest of an owl;
When they screamed in the nest, he screamed
out with the rest,
That depressing Old Person of Crowle.

Edward Lear

There was a Young Lady of Crowle
Who greeted the day with a scowl;
To approach was unsafe
When disturbing the waif,
So they poked her awake with a dowel.

A Lady of Winchelsea

There was an old Lady of Winchelsea,
Who said, "If you needle or pin shall see
On the floor of my room, sweep it up with the broom!"
That exhaustive old Lady of Winchelsea!

Edward Lear

Said the Pleasant Old Lady of Arches,
In a mood quite abnormally harsh,
"When you go to Winchelsea,
Say hello to Elsie,
And tell her to sit in the marsh!"

A Man In a Tree

There was an Old Man in a Tree,
Whose whiskers were lovely to see;
But the birds of the air pluck'd them perfectly
bare,
To make themselves nests in that tree.

   Edward Lear

There was an Old Man in a Tree,
But this time there wasn't a bee;
But a wasp and a hornet,
A cow with a cornet,
A deer and, I fear, a marquis.

There was an Old Man in a Tree

A Lady of Corsica

There was a Young Lady of Corsica,
Who purchased a little brown saucy-cur;
Which she fed upon ham, and hot raspberry
jam,
That expensive Young Lady of Corsica.

Edward Lear

There was a Young Lady of Corsica,
Who rode out one day on a horsica;
But with arms all a-paddle,
She fell from the saddle,
Her hem being caught in the gorsica.

A Lady of Firle

There was a Young Lady of Firle,
Whose hair was addicted to curl;
It curled up a tree, and all over the sea,
That expansive Young Lady of Firle.

Edward Lear

There was a Young Lady of Firle,
And life so mistreated the girl,
That however she'd arch them
Or pull them and starch them,
Her ringlets would never uncurl.

A Person of Stroud

There was an Old Person of Stroud,
Who was horribly jammed in a crowd;
Some she slew with a kick, some she scrunched with a stick,
That impulsive Old Person of Stroud.

Edward Lear

A Tumbling Person of Stroud
Came down with the rain from a cloud;
But a sheltering collie
Extended its brolly
To catch him, and gathered a crowd.

A Man of Boulak

There was an Old Man of Boulak,
Who sate on a Crocodile's back;
But they said, "Tow'rds the night he may
probably bite,
Which might vex you, Old Man of Boulak!"

Edward Lear

There was an Old Man of Boulak
Who was suddenly taken aback,
When the croc he was riding
Pulled in to a siding
And paused for a bit of a snack.

A Person of Skye

There was an Old Person of Skye,
Who waltz'd with a Bluebottle fly:
They buzz'd a sweet tune, to the light of the moon,
And entranced all the people of Skye.

Edward Lear

There was a Young Lady of Skye,
Whose future was written on high,
In a trail that said,
"Would you like to be wed?"
But she couldn't reach up to reply.

A Man of Blackheath

There was an Old Man of Blackheath,
Whose head was adorned with a wreath
Of lobsters and spice, pickled onions and mice,
That uncommon Old Man of Blackheath.

Edward Lear

A pirate near death in Blackheath
Wrote: "My treasure I hereby bequeath
To my dog and my cat,
And I buried it at ..."
But he ran out of ink underneath.

A Man, Who When Little

There was an Old Man, who when little
Fell casually into a kettle;
But, growing too stout, he could never get out,
So he passed all his life in that kettle.

Edward Lear

Baron Peanut was pleased on acquittal,
But the trial had rendered him brittle;
So the painted old gnome
Bore his fury, at home,
As it had since the Baron was little.

A Person of Dundalk

There was an Old Person of Dundalk,
Who tried to teach fishes to walk;
When they tumbled down dead, he grew weary, and said,
"I had better go back to Dundalk!"

Edward Lear

A Wordy Young Girl of Dundalk
Was determined that fishes would talk;
After years of research
She was left in the lurch,
Cause the fish had decided to walk.

A Person of Shoreham

There was an Old Person of Shoreham,
Whose habits were marked by decorum;
He bought an Umbrella, and sate in the cellar,
Which pleased all the people of Shoreham.

Edward Lear

There was an Old Person of Shoreham,
Who'd corner a victim and bore 'em
With a lengthy review
Of the knowledge he knew,
And there wasn't a lot of decorum.

A Person of Bar

There was an Old Person of Bar,
Who passed all her life in a jar,
Which she painted pea-green, to appear more serene,
That placid Old Person of Bar.

   Edward Lear

There was an Old Person of Bar,
Who shut himself up in a jar,
And secured a flight
Through a rip in the night
To a distant but welcoming star.

A Person of Kew

There was a Young Person of Kew,
Whose virtues and vices were few;
But with blameable haste she devoured some hot paste,
Which destroyed that Young Person of Kew.

Edward Lear

There was a Young Person of Kew,
Who went to the park to renew;
But the Covid restriction,
Applied with conviction,
Detained her all day in a queue.

A Person of Jodd

There was an Old Person of Jodd,
Whose ways were perplexing and odd;
She purchased a whistle, and sate on a thistle,
And squeaked to the people of Jodd.

Edward Lear

There was an Old Person of Jodd
Who always looked first where he trod,
Having noted before
That his cat had a claw,
And would use it if stepped on, the sod.

A Person of Bude

*There was an Old Person of Bude,
Whose deportment was vicious and crude;
He wore a large ruff of pale straw-coloured stuff,
Which perplexed all the people of Bude.*

Edward Lear

*There was a Young Lady of Bude
Who'd warned people not to intrude;
And those who, benighted,
Appeared uninvited,
Excited the girl to be rude.*

A Person of Brigg

There was an Old Person of Brigg,
Who purchased no end of a wig;
So that only his nose, and the end of his toes,
Could be seen when he walked about Brigg.

Edward Lear

There was an Old Lady of Brigg
Who simply could not give a fig,
Though she would offer parts
Of her salads and tarts
As the servings were often too big.

A Man of Messina

There was an Old Man of Messina,
Whose daughter was named Opsibeena;
She wore a small wig, and rode out on a pig,
To the perfect delight of Messina.

Edward Lear

Police came and got the Hyaena
As it played on an old ocarina,
And the charges confirm it -
To busk without permit
Will cost you a fine in Messina.

Police Came and Got the Hyaena

The Fifth Line

Limericks After Lear, Book One

The Fifth Line, Book One of Limericks After Lear, contains 112 new limericks based on Edward Lear's *A Book of Nonsense*.

Reviews

"The Fifth line: Limericks After Lear is a fun little book of limericks."

Flaka P, NetGalley Reviewer

"… I love reading limericks. They are funny, witty, and amusing. This book also embodies all these traits. The author has done a great job adapting the limericks and even made most of them better than the original."

Flaka P, NetGalley Reviewer

"… I would happily recommend the book to all poetry lovers or to people that enjoy reading limericks."

Flaka P, NetGalley Reviewer

"… So in this slender volume you get the original and the remake side by side to compare and decide which one you prefer. Plus some adorable black and white drawings."

Mia D, NetGalley Reviewer

"… Personally, I believe I liked the new versions more, they even made for an occasional laugh out loud moment. Though not like a proper laugh, more along the lines of a titter, snicker or a guffaw. But an adorable diversion, especially for fans of the jocular poetic art form that is a limerick."

Mia D, NetGalley Reviewer

"… A very quick read and a perfectly entertaining way to spend 35 minutes or so. Actually, I wish my brain was more awake right now, so I'd review this in a limerick format, but no…maybe at a later date. Yeah, fun was had. Recommended. Thanks NetGalley."

Mia D, NetGalley Reviewer

"… Yeah, fun was had. Recommended."

Mia D, NetGalley Reviewer

Sascha Martin's Rocket-Ship

"Misadventures have never been so much fun"

If you only have room for one catastrophe in your life this year, make it *Sascha Martin's Rocket-Ship*.

Reviews

5.0 out of 5 stars A joy to read!

"My sons and I absolutely LOVED this take on a science experiment gone wrong. It had a lot of humour, the rhyme was complex but worked well, and the illustrations were spot on! Misadventures have never been so much fun…"

Amazon Reviewer

5.0 out of 5 stars Really enjoyed the rhyming story.

"Hilarious, entertaining story, creative thinking, fun to read over and over again, imaginative, loved, loved, loved it, colorful pictures, wonderful science fiction"

Amazon Reviewer

5.0 out of 5 stars Great read!

"Short and sweet! Excellent book to read with my daughter and we loved all of the perfect rhyming and humor!"

Amazon Reviewer

5.0 out of 5 stars Very Entertaining!

"I found this book to be absolutely delightful! I read the book to myself and got a great chuckle out of the story."

Amazon Reviewer

5.0 out of 5 stars Great read

"Daughter loved it found it hilarious

"And cool she says"

Amazon Reviewer

5.0 out of 5 stars What a trip!

"A fun book to read. Certainly not a bedtime story, so full of action. My grandsons loved it."

Amazon Reviewer

5.0 out of 5 stars Super cute!

"I am 46 with no kids but I love children's books. This book was excellent! Very funny and wonderful artwork! I highly recommend for any age!"

Amazon Reviewer

5.0 out of 5 stars Hilariously
"Sascha Martin is so very very very funny…
"That's why I love this book so so much."
Amazon Reviewer

Thank You

Thanks for reading The Next Hundred Lears. I do hope you enjoyed the limericks, or some of them at least. If you're up for writing a review, that would be just ... amazing!!! ... because reviews help books (and me!) find new readers.

Discover More

Read more limericks, read about limericks, sign up for a newsletter, look in on the *Sascha Martin* books, or just reach out and say hi, all at ...

KidsBooke.com

www.ingramcontent.com/pod-product-compliance
Lightning Source LLC
Chambersburg PA
CBHW050317010526
44107CB00055B/2284